101 BEST EDUCATIONAL GAMES

GAMES TO LEARN BY

By
Muriel
Mandell

STERLING PUBLISHING CO., Inc.   New York

Oak Tree Press Co., Ltd. London & Sydney

OTHER BOOKS OF INTEREST

Best Singing Games for Children of
All Ages

Code Games

Hokus Pokus

101 Best Action Games for Boys

101 Best Games for Girls

101 Best Magic Tricks

Pantomimes, Charades and Skits

Puppet and Pantomime Plays

You Can Act!

Activities to Learn By

Dancing Games

Originally published and © 1958 by Sterling Publishing Co., Inc.
under the title "101 Best Educational Games"

Sixth Printing, 1975
Copyright © 1972 by Sterling Publishing Co., Inc.
419 Park Avenue South, New York, N.Y. 10016

Distributed in Australia and New Zealand by Oak Tree Press Co., Ltd.,
P.O. Box J34, Brickfield Hill, Sydney 2000, N.S.W.
Distributed in the United Kingdom and elsewhere in the British Commonwealth
by Ward Lock Ltd., 116 Baker Street, London W 1
Manufactured in the United States of America
Library of Congress Catalog Card No.: 58-12540
Sterling ISBN 0-8069-4520-6 Trade   Oak Tree 7061-2391-3
4521-4 Library

Table of Contents

Before You Begin

Games carry their own built-in motivation for use by those of us—parents, teachers and group leaders—who are concerned with educating children

We need not wait for either a classroom or a party situation to couple knowledge and fun. A parent can make a long city walk more interesting for preschool children by looking for things that "start like boy," or by scouting for the letter "*B*" in the street and store signs. Travelling in a bus or a car, family members can challenge one another to sight red cars or certain license plates, birch trees or three-storey buildings. These informal games provide painless practice in hearing and seeing differences, skills essential for readying a child to learn to read.

On a more formal level, *Scrabble* and *Anagrams* build vocabulary and provoke dictionary use by 8-year-olds and 80-year-olds.

Because much of the problem of learning is attitude, games are particularly useful in helping the reluctant learner and the child in need of remedial work, to overcome resistance toward a particular field. The fearful or rebellious, the bored or the slow often participate enthusiastically in a learning game, which then serves as a powerful incentive for learning.

After a chapter of icebreakers, culled from the various fields to help young people to socialize, the games in this book are divided into chapters according to subject matter, as it is organized in most elementary schools.

The subjects, of course, overlap and some of the games classified as social studies might easily fall into mathematics or science. Similarly, some of the game devices listed for one field can easily be utilized for another. Social studies games readily convert to spelling games by replacing history and geography questions with spelling words. *Crossword Puzzles* can become

Crossmath Puzzles by replacing verbal questions with those requiring numerical answers.

Each of the chapters starts with the simplest games of the particular subject matter, usually utilizing physical activity or dramatic play. These are designed for the 6- and 7-year-old, though many are still useful (sometimes with a few variations) for the older child.

Next come more involved games for the 8- to 10-year-old, games which teach specific learnings, require more skills, or call for more mature reactions. Some of the games are suitable for the teenager in need of remediation.

In some instances, games such as *Word Lotto* provide tests of knowledge without the stress of formal testing. In others, games relieve the tedium of drill—*Tick-Tock* gives practice in telling time; *Numbers Line-Up* effectively places value. *Bingo,* commercial or homemade, leads to facility in number reading.

Other games are calculated to encourage a logical method of approach, to promote thought, whatever the special field of study. These exist for every age level from *I'm Thinking of a Color* to *Phenomena.*

It is important that each game be geared to each child's individual needs and to his level of skill and maturity. If more than one child is involved, each must compete at his own "weight." If uneven players are to be matched, the superior player must be "handicapped" so that each child can perform successfully. *Spelling Golf* shows one way of solving this dilemma.

Particularly for the 6- to 8-year-old, and for the reluctant or slow learner as well, competition must be underplayed. Scoring is not always necessary; it is rarely a factor when the game is just introduced. When possible, the children should keep score themselves and also serve as referees. These tasks often prove as valuable as playing and almost as much fun. An adult observer, however, is advisable at least until the players are adept enough to play independently.

Let *games* show you that learning—and teaching—can be fun!

1. Icebreakers

BETTY'S APPLES

Players of all ages will enjoy this game which presents a challenging code to decipher.

The leader says: "Betty likes apples but hates pears. What do you like?"

If the answer is, "I like peaches," the leader says, "I'm sorry. You didn't get the message. Jessie likes ballet but hates modern dance. What do you like?"

If the answer is "lettuce" or "football," the leader says: "You may send the answering message."

And the answering message might well be, "Henny likes jelly but hates jam."

The code, of course, involves the double letter in the liked objects, apples, ballet, lettuce, football.

When most of the players have broken the code, it's time for a new code—perhaps a word ending in "able" this time.

CUT-OUT CAPERS

Any group of young detectives will find it hard to stay aloof from one another in the wake of this assignment.

Cut out photographs from newspapers and magazines and mount them on cardboard. Then cut each in two in irregular fashion. Mix up the pieces.

Hand one of these jagged parts to each of the players and set each to unearth his severed segment.

Try to choose interesting news photos for children aged 9 to 10. Then when two players have joined together what your scissors have torn asunder, they can tackle the photograph's caption and learn something of current events.

TALKING CONTEST

If the group includes shy children or if speaking before the group is coming hard for some, try unloosening their tongues with this icebreaker. It may not make sense, but then it isn't meant to.

Assign two children topics of interest — anything from "Do you believe in Santa Claus?" to "Is there life on Mars?" At a signal, the two must face one another and begin talking. Each must make himself heard and continue to talk, as quickly as possible and without hesitating, for 30 seconds.

FIND THE FOOD

To help the 6- and 7-year-old over the hurdle of meeting a large number of strange children, divide the group into animal families of 5 or 6.

Assign an appropriate color to each family: red to the cows, gray to the donkeys, yellow to the chickens, brown to the horses. Then let each group draw lots for a leader. (The child picking the short slip can be the leader.)

While the drawing is going on, hide colored squares of paper about the room. Then set the animals to find food — in the form of the paper of their particular color. When a cow comes upon any square, no matter the color, she moos until her leader comes. The leader collects the paper if it is red or destroys it if it is enemy food, that is, another color. Similarly, a donkey brays, a chicken clucks and a horse neighs to announce a discovery. Each leader then collects or destroys the square depending on its color.

After time is called (10 minutes is ample), the squares are counted. The group with the largest number of squares of the right color is entitled to more human fare, possibly in the form of ice cream or candy.

SAM SMITH'S SUITCASE

The first or second time a group gets together, try this game to catch the attention of all the children and set them thinking.

The leader says: "My name is Sam Smith. I'm going to take a trip and take along a suitcase. I'll take some of you with me — but only if you take the right thing with you. Remember, I'm going to take a suitcase."

Each of the young players is then asked what he will take along. Thomas says: "My name is Thomas and I will take along ties." "You may come," says Mr. Smith. Jane says: "My name is Jane. I'll bring along a ribbon." "I'm sorry," says Mr. Smith, "you must stay home this trip."

Those who name objects that begin with the first letter of their name are the only ones to be taken along.

But be sure to go on a second trip so that those who couldn't go the first time get a chance to make the journey.

Jane	Lenny	Harry	Ann
Mary	Elliot	Mark	Edgar
Dan	Ellen	Andy	Jon
Sara	Jean	Tad	Karen

NAME GAME

When a group first gets together, Name Game is a handy way of introducing the children to one another and perhaps of speeding the learning of each other's names. It can be played with as few as 9 or as many as 40.

Each child writes or prints his name on a small slip of paper, which is collected and put into a small box or bowl.

Then large sheets of paper (8½ x 11 will do) are handed to the children and each is directed to fold or rule the sheet into squares — either 3, 4, 5 or 6 squares in each direction (depending on the number of players).

Once the chart is prepared, all of the children, armed with their charts, approach the others and ask their first names. They write or print these on their charts in any box, obtaining as many different names as there are squares. (Unless there are exactly 9, 16, 25 or 36 children, not every child's name will be on every chart.) The children should be divided to start their name collecting from alternate sides of the room. Allow adequate time for this name collecting. After all, the whole idea is for the children to get to know one another.

When the name collecting is ended, hand out one sheet of colored construction paper to each child. He then prepares 15 or 20 small colored squares, the same size as the squares on his chart. If the group is small, he will need fewer squares.

When charts and colored squares are ready, the leader draws out one of the slips from the box and calls the name written on it. The child whose name is called identifies himself (perhaps adding his last name). Any player who has the name on his chart places one of the colored squares over it. The leader continues to draw until at least one player covers all the names in a row, either vertically, horizontally or diagonally. When this happens, the winning player shouts "Name Game!"

To play the game again, each player merely clears his chart and the leader puts the name slips back into the box.

HIDDEN WORD

Divide a group of good readers (if you have them) into twosomes and start them playing Hidden Word, a guaranteed warmer-upper.

Using the equipment and junk hidden in pockets and purses, or in desks and about the room, each partner in turn lines up three or four items (on a table or desk or on the floor). The other player must form a word from the initial letter of each article. He may be given a hint that the word is an animal or color, for instance.

One partner may line up a book, a letter, an apple, a crayon, a key, with the word *black* in mind. The other may array a clip, orange and a watch to form cow.

After an allotted time, items go back into hiding. Children change partners and set up words again.

Usually, the fun of meeting and challenging one another is incentive enough, but if scoring is desired, allow a point for each correct "discovery" of a hidden word.

THE PUNCTUATION STORY

Assign sounds for punctuation marks before a story is to be read. For example, for a period — clap hands; comma — snap fingers; quotation marks — two clucks of the tongue; question mark — dog yip; exclamation point — whistle; hyphen — foot stamp; apostrophe — snore.

Each child should have a copy of the story to follow as it is being read aloud.

Any story with dialogue will do, but a funny story becomes even funnier. At the start, announce the punctuation marks as you would in proofreading. For example, say: "Quote Where are you going comma Johnny question quote asked his mother period." The children will willy-nilly become aware of punctuation, and as they get to know it, you can change your reading method so they remind you of the marks.

For the younger children, the leader may do the reading, but most 8-, 9- and 10-year-olds will enjoy reading and punctuating by themselves. If the group is large, you can divide it into teams, each team being held responsible for a particular punctuation mark, and the captains sharing the reading.

After the first few times, the children will want to devise their own punctuation code.

WORD MATE

Because it gives the children an opportunity to pair off on the basis of mutual interest, Word Mate is an excellent icebreaker providing both learning and fun.

Prepare for the game by printing small words on cards (4 x 6 or larger). Use such words as *some, any, every* and *thing, body, time,* which combine in a variety of ways to make simple compound words.

Give each child one card. Each player is to find a partner with another word with which he can build a new word. In some cases there will be only one possible mate with whom a player can get together; in others, there will be several possibilities.

Other Word Mate suggestions: *step, ladder; waste, basket; base, ball; smoke, stack; foot, print; grand, mother; barn, yard; may, be; store, room, black, board,* etc.

2. Music, Art and Puppetry Games

RHYTHM MIMES

Collect percussion or simple melody instruments for each of the players but one. These can be drums, tambourines, rattles, triangles, bells, etc. If you don't have enough, it's fun to make them from odds and ends — pots, boxes, blocks, sticks, tin cans, spoons, whisk brooms, coins, and cord.*

Draw lots for the various instruments. The one with the blank paper is "It."

"It" claps a rhythm, and then points to one of the others to reproduce the rhythm on his instrument. First to miss becomes "It" for the next round.

If no one misses, "It" is still "It" — and he'd better make the rhythm more complicated! And the leader had better listen and observe carefully!

---

* See *Make Your Own Musical Instruments* by Mandell and Wood.

SIMONOVITCH PLAYS

Simonovitch Plays will help youngsters learn to *listen* to the timbre of various instruments. The larger the group, the more the fun.

Each of the players may have a percussion or makeshift instrument or simply be instructed to clap, stamp or tap on a floor, table or desk with hands or a ruler.

The leader is equipped with two instruments — bells and a triangle, tambourine and a drum, piano and xylophone, or, for a more difficult game, two drums, two rattles or two horns, of different pitch.

One of the leader's two instruments is "Simonovitch," and the group is so informed. If "Simonovitch" plays a rhythm, so do the other players. If the leader's other instrument plays, no one else does. Anyone who plays at the wrong time, or does not play at the right time, is out.

GUESS THE SONG

Hand-clapping or foot-stamping will do for this rhythm game, but it is even more fun with simple percussion instruments.

One player taps out the rhythm of a song familiar to the group. The others try to guess the name. The successful guesser taps out the next song.

A group of 9- or 10-year-olds may split into two bands. One band taps out (in unison, of course) a rhythm for the players of the other band to guess.

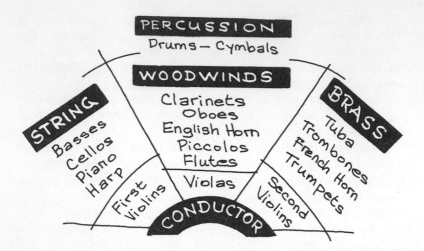

ORCHESTRA

Once the children know a little about the various instruments that make up an orchestra, show them how to play the game of Orchestra. A large group makes this old favorite more fun and permits better teaching.

Divide the group into string, wind, brass and percussion families. Then assign each player a particular instrument to pantomime. Seat the families properly, as in the diagram, to give to the game a feeling of a real orchestra. Working with 20 players, assign 11 string (4 first violins, 4 second violins, 2 cellos, 1 bass); 2 woodwind (2 clarinets); 5 brass (2 French horns, 2 trumpets, 1 trombone); and 2 percussion (1 bass drum, and 1 snare drum and cymbals).

If your group is larger, include 4 violas and additional strings (possibly 4 violins, 2 cellos, 2 basses); add a flute and an oboe to the wind section and an upright bass to the brass. You can divide the chore of percussion instruments among several players. Be sure each child knows exactly how his instrument is played.

The leader, as conductor, sings a familiar song and at the same time plays an instrument in pantomime. He may choose any instrument in the orchestra. Each player pantomimes his own instrument but watches the conductor carefully. The conductor suddenly changes his pantomime to another instrument. That is the signal for the child (or children) playing that instrument to switch to the conductor's previous instrument.

For instance, if the leader starts by "playing" the piano and then switches to the drum, the drummers must pantomime the piano. When the conductor switches back to piano or to a third instrument, the drummers go back to drumming and the game continues.

DO RE ME

To help a group become more familiar with written musical symbols, try Do Re Me. Groups of 7, 14 and 21 can play.

Seven players are seated in a circle or in a row. Each is given a slip of paper on which is written a C scale with one note identified, by number, letter or Italian name. (Each player has a different note.) It might look like this:

The leader starts the group on movements in rhythm, perhaps a ¾-time *snap fingers, clap hands, slap lap.* He waits until all the players are moving rhythmically with him. Then the leader sings out the name of a note as all *slap lap*. If he sings out "D," for instance, "D" must respond by calling out another note by the third beat, that is, by the time the group has repeated *snap fingers, clap hands, slap lap*. This next player in turn must respond by calling out another note before the next *snap fingers, clap hands, slap lap,* have been completed.

As soon as the children get over their confusion and their shyness, each player can be required to sing out the note (correctly, if possible) as he names it.

Color Games

While most 6- and 7-year-olds know the primary colors, many have trouble identifying some of the others. Brown and black are confused, gray and tan are interchanged, and unknown are navy, purple, chartreuse, aqua and coral. But whether the problem is to establish the basic colors or to encourage further color discrimination, these color games will help.

I'M THINKING OF A COLOR

One of the players quietly selects an object and whispers its identity to the leader (or prints the name on a piece of paper). The child then says to the group, "I'm thinking of something in this room and it is red." Of course, he does not look at the object he has selected.

The other players take turns trying to identify the object by asking questions that can be answered only by "yes" or "no." As long as the answer is "yes," the same child continues his questioning. When the answer is "no," the next player has a turn.

With the guidance of the leader, the children will soon learn to make their first questions general and then move on to specific items.

An inexperienced player asks, "Is it Jerry's red shirt?" If he is wrong, he will learn only that it is not Jerry's shirt. Later, this same player will learn that it is smarter to ask, "Is it something to wear?" With this one question, if the answer is "no," he will learn that the object is not Jerry's shirt, Donald's tie, Mark's socks or Mary's dress.

The child who guesses correctly chooses the next object and again tells only its color.

Teams for 9 and 10

This can be particularly enjoyable as a team game for 9- and 10-year-olds. Members of one team select an object which members of the other team take turns trying to guess. There is an incentive to make the questions meaningful, for if the object is not guessed by the time all the members of the team have had a turn, the answer is disclosed and the same team selects the next object.

Ten-year-olds enjoy adding the challenge of using synonyms (raven instead of black, cherry or cerise for red, etc.) or ingredients (red-and-yellow for orange or blue-and-yellow for green). This may call for a little artbook or dictionary consultation, certainly a practice to be encouraged.

COLOR RELAY

From oaktag or cardboard, cut out identical sets of fruit forms (bananas, apples, oranges, grapes, plums, etc.). Mount each set on a separate large sheet of wrapping paper. Tack or tape the wrapping papers to the wall, far enough apart so that the children can color without interfering with one another.

Divide the group into teams and line them up. In a classroom, children can start the game from their seats and each row can be a separate team.

Hand a box of crayons to the first child of each team. At the signal, each dashes up and colors any one of the fruit forms with the appropriate crayon. When he is finished, he hurries the box of crayons to the next player on his team. Dropped crayons must be picked up by the racing player, not by teammates.

The winning team is the first to complete the set of forms correctly.

Forms could be vegetables, animals or birds.

COLOR COLLECTOR

In a box or bowl, mix 5-inch squares of different colored construction paper. For real efficiency, staple or paste the squares on 8½ x 11 sheets of plain white paper.

If the group is large, divide it into teams of 4 or 5 players. Each player or team leader chooses a square from the box. Then the players set out to find all the items of the assigned color that are in the room.

Younger children may report their findings to an adult for help in recording, but 8-, 9- and 10-year-olds can be expected to keep their own lists on the reverse side of their colored squares or sheets.

After an allotted time (10 minutes is usually ample and shorter periods are sometimes more challenging), lists are collected and each is read aloud. After each reading, the teams are allowed 30 seconds in which to point out items of other teams' colors that have not been already mentioned. For instance, the "red" team might turn up a yellow handkerchief peeping from the pocket of a member of the "yellow" team!

FORM FUN

Jigsaw puzzles also give a sense of size and shape, of parts and the whole, and develop both manual and mental skills. Form Fun, in addition, introduces area relationships the youngsters will later meet in geometry.

Trace the parts illustrated on cardboard or paper. Assemble them to form the figure indicated:

THE CIRCLE

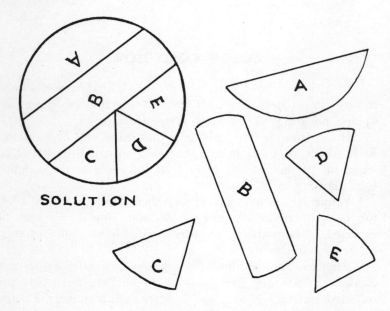

SOLUTION

THE TRIANGLE

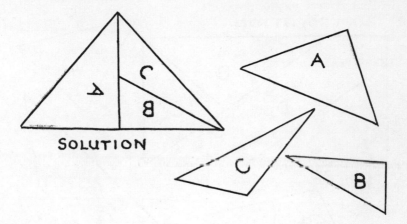

SOLUTION

THE RECTANGLE

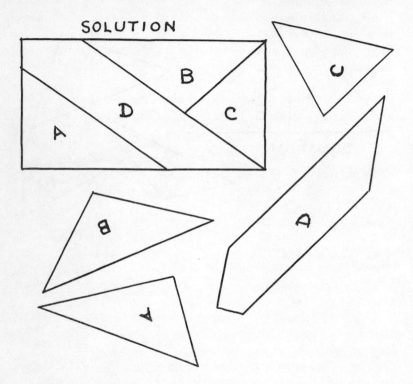

SOLUTION

DRAW THE ELEPHANT'S TAIL

This version of that old party favorite, Pin-on-the-Donkey's-Tail, requires the blindfolded player to draw in an appropriate tail at an appropriate place.

Draw a figure of a pig or elephant or cat on a large sheet of wrapping paper. Mark the place where the tail should be. Supply each player with a crayon of a different color. Blindfold the player, turn him around three times, and send him forth to draw.

For variations, blindfolded players can supply a stem for an apple, a nose for a face, a doorknob for a door.

ART CHARADES

With the incentive of making themselves understood, youngsters — who tend to grow inhibited artistically as they get older — relax their suspicions of sketch pad and crayon. Any number from 4 to 40 can turn artist.

Divide the group into two teams and designate one team as challenger and the other as the guessing team.

The challenging team selects a word or title with literary, historical or geographical allusions. The choice — *Goldilocks*, for instance — is written on a slip of paper.

One member of the guessing team reports to the challengers and receives the slip on which word or title is written. (In the case of beginning readers it might be better to substitute whispering. Though the artist might be able to *read* the title, chances are the challenging team would have trouble *writing* it!)

Returning to his team in the guise of artist, it is up to the child to try to indicate the word or title by drawing appropriate pictures. In the case of *Goldilocks* he may outline three bears before he sketches in a little girl. While he draws, his team tries to guess the charade within an allotted time.

If the team guesses the correct word or title, they choose the next word for the other team to draw and guess. Otherwise, the same team selects the next word but another player is the artist.

SCULPTURE EXHIBIT

Most youngsters love to work with clay, but freeze at the necessity of creating an assigned object. Sculpture Exhibit sidetracks that problem and encourages each to mold what he will.

Seat the children at a table, or in a circle on the floor. Protect the area with oilcloth or newspaper. Then in front of each child put a mound of clay, and an assortment of toothpicks, corks, pipecleaners, acorns, pine cones or nuts.

Tell the children they have 5 (or 10) minutes in which to make anything they choose — abstract or representational. When time is called, place at the base of each "statue" a sheet of paper (8 x 10). Tack the paper down at the bottom. Each sculptor is to jot down a title for his work at the top of the sheet, and then fold it over. Then each sculptor works his way around the table giving a title to his fellow artists' works, being sure to fold down the paper before he goes on to the next. When every sculptor has titled every piece of sculpture the sheets are unfolded and read aloud.

Puppets

More and more elementary schools are saying "open sesame" to the ancient art of puppetry, with the increasing recognition of its value as a means of stimulating children to communicate their ideas and feelings.

Moreover, puppet magic can be used to animate and illuminate many fields of learning — speaking, reading, creative writing, literature, music, history, geography, science and mathematics.

There are many kinds of finger and hand puppets that the 6- to 10-year-old will find both easy to make and to manipulate. Here are a few examples with some applications.

PEANUT PUPPETS

Puppets made from peanut shell halves are among the simplest. They can be manipulated by the 6- and 7-year-old, for dramatic play and learning games. One child alone or any number can play.

The child just draws in eyes, nose and mouth on the shells and fits them on the tips of his fingers. To present a show, he can put his hands below the edge of the table, letting his puppet-capped fingers stick up. For a more elaborate stage, remove a piece from the top and bottom of a kitchen match box, as in the illustration. On with the show.

COUNT NOSES

Count Noses is a counting game for two puppeteers to play with their peanut puppets. Both puppeteers hide their people below the table. At the signal (One, two, three"), each puppeteer sends onto the stage as many puppets as he wishes — merely by sticking up his peanut-topped fingers. Each player tries to be the first to call out the correct number of all the puppets on stage.

PAPER PLATE PUPPET

Paper plate puppets require slightly more skill to make than peanut puppets. They make fine projects for the 6- to 8-year-old.

Two plates are needed for each puppet. On the bottom of one plate, the young puppeteer draws a face and pastes on a headdress of crepe paper or a few strands of yarn or cotton for hair. He can easily make a witch or Santa Claus, a policeman or fireman, a clown or a fairy.

Then the two plates are stapled or taped together, bottom sides out. On the blank plate, the child cuts a slit or small hole large enough for him to be able to fit in two or three fingers. His wrist then serves as a neck.

HOLIDAY GAME

Holiday Game is a good social studies individual or team game to play with paper plate puppets.

If the group is large, divide it into small companies. Assign to each puppeteer or company of puppeteers a particular holiday for which to make puppets. When the puppets are completed, they should enact a suitable scene and the others try to guess the holiday.

One little group might use an Indian puppet showing a Pilgrim puppet how to plant corn, to illustrate Thanksgiving. Dialogue is not out of order, but the name of the holiday should not be mentioned.

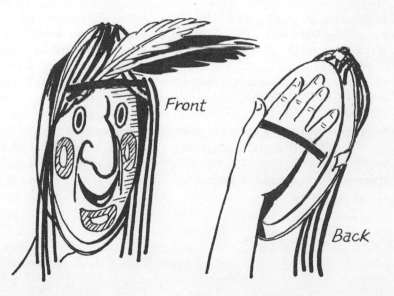

Front

Back

3. Language Arts Games

THE SOUNDS OF THINGS

To help the beginning reader, here is a version with the emphasis on the initial *sound* rather than on the alphabetical name. One or many may play.

The player says, "I'm thinking of something to drink that starts like monkey." The others guess until one correctly calls "milk." The next player, perhaps, says, "I'm thinking of a day of the week that starts like father" and others guess until one says "Friday." Later the players can choose objects that start like "cherry" or "Thursday" or "string" and the players will be challenged to reproduce the more complicated sounds.

To give the beginner experience with the final sound of a word, the player says: "I'm thinking of a word that means something you bounce and it rhymes with wall."

SIMON SAYS

tested Simon Says can help increase English
or introduce a foreign language. It's been particularly
s an aid in teaching English to non-English-speaking

est to have an adult serve as leader but you need
e number of children playing. If space is a problem,
vities to those that require only a small area.
ader stands facing the group. Station the children
t as space permits. In a classroom, they can remain
ecessary.
me is played this way: The leader puts his hand

The arts of listening carefull
put to the test with a fast game o
8 to 40 can play.

If the group is large enough,
the players of each team in a circ
and decide on a one-sentence mes
weatherman says it is going to rai
is the capital of New York State."
on two slips of paper, return to the
each hands the slip, folded with
player on his *left*.

Then each leader whispers
his *right*. This player whispers
who whispers to his neighbor or
around to the last person in the

When both teams are finishe
repeats aloud the message he h
slip and reads the original mes
message more nearly correct, sco

For the next game, the la
and decide on the next message

Winning team is the one w
player has had a chance to com

Time-
vocabulary
successful
children.

It is
not limit t
restrict act

The l
as far apar
seated, if n

The g

on his head saying "Simon says, 'Hands on your head.'" Each player must put his hands on his head. The leader says next, "Simon says, 'Wiggle your fingers.' Open your mouth." Each child then wiggles his fingers — but does not open his mouth. Why? Because that command was not immediately preceded by the words "Simon Says." He must obey only orders that "Simon Says" or he is out. In each case, the leader can act out the directions himself or try to fool the players by doing something entirely different, moving his legs when he says arms, etc.

When Simon Says is used to increase vocabulary, the leader can introduce words ranging from shin to chin, from thigh to clavicle, from leap to squat. For the first few times he uses a new word, the leader should match his actions with the directions. There should be no attempt to "fool" the group until the word's meaning is well established. Later, such high jinks will serve as a good test.

Similarly, in teaching a foreign language, a leader says, for instance, "Simon dit: les mains sur la tete" or "Simon dice: las manos encima de la cabeza." This need not be coupled with the English but the leader should match his own actions to the words until the group is sure of the meaning.

Because in each instance Simon Says gives an immediate use for the vocabulary, it serves as an incentive to rapid learning and retention.

ACTING NURSERY RHYMES

To provide an opportunity for dramatic play, divide the group into two or more acting companies. Let each decide on a nursery rhyme and then act it out for the others to guess. Actors can use both pantomime and dialogue.

"Mary Had a Little Lamb" is a good recommendation for one of the larger groups because it calls for a good-sized cast including Mary, her lamb, the teacher, and Mary's schoolmates. You might remind the children also of "Sing a Song of Sixpence" (with its "four and twenty blackbirds") and "Humpty-Dumpty" (with "all the King's horses and all the King's men").

Small acting companies will do well with "Old Mother Hubbard," "Little Miss Muffet," "Jack and Jill," "The Queen of Hearts," or "The Three Little Kittens."

Older children can select other literary situations to reproduce — perhaps scenes from "Cinderella," "Jack and the Beanstalk," "The Boy Who Cried Wolf," etc.

AND THEN . . .

Long before children develop enough skill to write independently, the cooperatively-composed story is a source of stimulation and entertainment. It's a fine method for increasing vocabulary while sparking imagination.

The leader starts the story with an appropriate situation but stops at a crucial moment and turns the narration over to one of the children with ". . . and then . . ." Each child in turn adds a crisis or two until the last draws the story to a satisfactory conclusion.

Most 6- and 7-year-olds do better when dealing with a story of children their own age in realistic surroundings, but older youngsters are stirred to creativity by fairies and supermen. Don't be surprised if Annie Oakley downs the Wicked Queen or Mighty Mouse takes on the fierce Giant.

Horse	Run
Three	Went
Squirrel	House
There	Want
Ran	The

House

Horse

WORD LOTTO GAME

Many word lotto games are on the market but most are neither as much fun nor as versatile a reading aid as the homemade variety. You can make word cards on different reading levels, replace last month's set with a new one that includes the new word list, and provide for any number of players.

Making the Game

For each player, supply two pieces of stiff cardboard about 6 inches wide and 8 inches long. Direct the children to divide each card in half lengthwise and then to further divide it into five horizontal spaces, as in the diagram.

Supply a word list (or use the one at the back of a reader) from which players may select *any* 10 words to print wherever they wish in the spaces on one of their cards.

On the second cardboard, each player prints the same words

as on his first card, then cuts along the lines so that he has 10 word slips. These are given to the leader, who assembles the word slips so that any duplicates are together.

The leader then collects the cards.

Playing the Game

One card is given to each player.

From the pile of assembled word slips, the leader picks up one slip at random and calls out the word. Each player looks for the word on his card. If he finds it, he reports to the leader for the slip with which to cover it. The leader will have enough duplicates to supply all the players who have the word on their cards, but he will not offer the slip to any player who does not ask for it. He will just put aside the uncalled-for slips and go on to the next word.

The player who first covers all the words on his card wins the game.

If the leader has slips left at the end of the game, he knows those are the words that are giving particular trouble. He will make sure they are included in the next game.

Beginners' Lotto

For beginners, paste above each word on the card an appropriate picture cut from a magazine or newspaper.

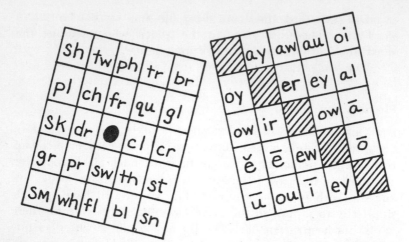

PHONICS LOTTO

For the child, whatever his age, who is having trouble distinguishing the sounds of letters, Phonics Lotto is one of the answers, particularly for the foreign-language child learning English. Commercial versions are available, but again tailor-made ones are more adaptable.

Ordinary 3" x 5" index cards are perfect, but oaktag or cardboard will also do. Divide each card into five vertical columns and then divide each column into five horizontally. At random, scatter the letters of the alphabet in each square leaving the middle one free. If there are particular sounds that the child has trouble with, be sure these are included on all the cards.

The backs of these cards, or other cards, might be filled separately with the more difficult consonant combinations—the blends—such as sh, ch, tr, fr, pl, gr, cl, dr, br, st, wh, etc. Or a series may be made of vowels and vowel combinations.

Also prepare several dozen blank squares to serve as counters.

Each child is given one or two cards, depending on his level of skill. The leader calls off three or four words beginning with the same sound (or ending with the same sound, if it is final sound that needs the practice). The leader calls out, "First, fan, father." The player who recognizes the sound and locates the symbol on his card calls out, "I have it." He receives one of the small squares to cover his letter. Game object is to be first to cover five squares vertically, horizontally or diagonally. Real object, of course, is to acquire sound and symbol familiarity.

SPELLING GOLF

With the increasing popularity of golf on the national scene, Spelling Golf well fits the need for a new game to review a lesson, introduce new words or just have spelling fun. Any number from 10 to 40 can play.

As in regulation golf, the course has 9 or 18 holes, but in this case the "holes" are words. The game consists of spelling those words in as few "strokes" (or players) as are needed to get into the "hole" — that is, to obtain the correct spelling of the word.

Divide the group into two teams, and line them up on opposite sides of the room. It isn't necessary for the teams to be equal in number. You may split the group so that an equal number of good and poor spellers are on each team. Or you may put all those on one level of spelling on one team, and those on another level of spelling on the other. Each team will be "stroking" at words appropriate to its own development. This game, thus, has an advantage over other spelling games in that both poor and good spellers have opportunities to shine.

The leader has a list of 18 or 36 words, either 9 or 18 for each team, so that each team plays either 9 or 18 "holes," depending on the length of time available for the game.

The leader calls off a word for the first player on Team A to drive. If he spells the word correctly, his team has made a hole in 1. If he does not, each partner on the *same* team takes a turn spelling the word until someone spells it correctly. The number of players it takes to spell the word is the number of "strokes" recorded for that hole. (See the diagram.)

Once the first hole is made the other team takes its place on the tee to shoot for hole 1. The leader calls out a word for the first player of Team B (either of similar difficulty or of lesser difficulty depending on how the group was divided). Recorded again are the number of strokes or players it takes to spell the word.

The leader then goes back to the players of Team A with

Score card for Team A		
Hole	**Strokes**	
1	~~HHH~~ ‖	= 7
2	‖‖	= 3
3	‖	= 2
4	⎮	= 1
5		
6		
7		
8		
9		
	Total	

another word for hole 2. First to drive would be a player who has not yet spelled. If it has taken six players to spell the team's first word, then the seventh player shoots for the team's second word. When each of the players of a team has spelled, start again at the beginning of the line of players.

After 9 or 18 holes are played by both sides, the team with the lowest score becomes the champion.

MYSTERY STORY

Challenged to solve the "mystery" of who did it, children are encouraged to recall story ideas, facts and details, and they may also be stimulated to broaden their reading practices.

This is one quiz game that parent and child can play in a bus or car quite readily, but is even more fun when a large group is participating.

The game is started by parent or leader asking a question about the identity of a character from a story or rhyme. Of course, it must be someone from among the literary acquaintances of the children. Here are some examples:

Who went fast asleep when he should have been working? (Little Boy Blue)

Who entered a strange house, broke up the furniture, ate the food, and fled when the owners came home? (Goldilocks)

Who broke a promise and stayed out late? (Cinderella)

Who took a friend along to school against the rules? (Mary)

Who stole some tarts? (The Knave of Hearts)

The first player to "find" the culprit gets the opportunity to tell the whole story of the "crime" and then to pose the next mystery.

cautious · coy · curly

THE DOCTOR'S CAT

The Doctor's Cat is a memory game requiring each player to use an adjective beginning with the same initial letter to describe the cat.

The children sit in a circle. The first player says, "The doctor's cat is an active cat." The second says, "The doctor's cat is an active, angry cat." After each player adds an adjective beginning with "a," the sentence returns to the first player, who then makes a descriptive remark about the cat beginning with "b."

If the game is to be a learning device, the meaning of the adjective must be a factor and no adjective should be accepted that could not be descriptive of a cat.

For the 7- and 8-year-old player, it may be advisable to go from the first player's "active cat" to a second player's "active big cat" and the third's "active, big, clever cat," etc.

COFFEEPOT

Even before the formal study of parts of speech, children can evolve a concept of the action word or verb of the sentence by playing Coffeepot. Any number from 2 to 40 can play.

While one of the players is out of the room, the others decide on a verb, such as "eat." Then the player returns and tries to guess the verb by asking questions which can be answered by "yes" or "no." Working from general questions, the player gradually narrows down the possibilities.

Do animals coffeepot? — Yes.

Do all people coffeepot? — Yes.

Do we coffeepot standing up? — Yes and no.

Do you *like* to coffeepot? — Yes.

Do you coffeepot in the morning? — Yes.

After a few games of Coffeepot, you'll be taken aback by the speed with which 8-, 9- and 10-year-olds track down a particular verb. And furthermore, they learn exactly what word in a sentence is the verb.

NEXT WORD?

This is a game bound to trick the wool-gatherer, but it can stump even the most attentive of listeners. Any number can play. A large group, however, should be divided into teams.

The leader reads aloud a story or article but pauses either in the middle or toward the end of a sentence to ask, "Next word?" Individual players or teams take turns supplying a word. The first to give the correct "next word" scores a point. The winner is the player or team with the most points at the end of the story.

WHY, WHEN, WHERE?

Why, When, Where? involves tracking down an unknown noun in a manner somewhat different from the verb-sleuthing of Coffeepot, but it serves a similar learning purpose for the name words of the language.

One player leaves the room while the others decide on a person, place or thing. No proper nouns are permitted. The group may select "bread," for instance.

When the player returns, he can ask the following questions:

Question: WHEN do you use it?
Answer: Several times a day.
Question: WHY do you use it?
Answer: It tastes good.
Question: WHERE do you use it?
Answer: In the kitchen.

The player can ask the same questions of each of the players, who must give him different answers. He continues until he guesses the noun or gives up. Someone else then leaves the room and the group chooses a new name word.

ADVERBS

On a par with Coffeepot as an early grammar lesson is Adverbs, the game that requires players to guess "how" an action is performed. Any number can play.

One player selects an adverb, such as "quickly." The others try to guess as each asks "It" to do some particular act in the manner of the adverb. For example, the first player may say, "Dress in the manner of the adverb." "It" must then pantomime dressing quickly. As other players request that he "move in the manner of the adverb" or "eat in the manner of the adverb" he must do these actions quickly. Each player in turn requests some act in the manner of the adverb until one guesses what the adverb is.

If one of the young players guesses a synonym it is acceptable. (For "quickly," accept "fast," "swiftly" or "rapidly.") The player who guesses the adverb becomes "It" and has a chance to select the next adverb.

Variation

Adverbs is often played in reverse fashion — one player guessing the adverb that the group has chosen. This has the advantage of allowing each of the players to pantomime an action, but it is more difficult for the one young player to guess than for the group.

BLACKBOARD RELAY

A painless way to give practice in sentence structure is the Blackboard Relay. If no blackboard is available, tack a large sheet of wrapping paper to the wall. From 6 to 40 can participate in the same race.

Divide the group into two or more teams and line them up at the back of the room, some distance from the board. In a classroom, each row of seats can be a team and the race can start from the seats. Give the first player of each team a piece of chalk (or pencil).

At the signal, the first player of each team runs to the board, writes or prints a word as legibly as possible, then dashes back and hands the chalk to the player next in line.

The second player runs to the board and adds a word, either in front of or after the first word. He returns to his line, hands the chalk to the third player, and the procedure is repeated. Each must avoid completing the sentence before the last player on his team has run. In addition to writing a word, this last player must also put in any capitalization and punctuation required.

The team that finishes first with a complete sentence scores. For the 10-year-olds, give double score for complex or compound sentences.

RIME TIME

For the 9- and 10-year-old, Rime Time is a fascinating game. Two can play but a large group makes for a faster moving game.

One player chooses a word and says: "I'm thinking of a word that rhymes . . . with fame."

Another player responds with: "Is it what a person is called?"

"It" says: "No, it is not a name."

A third player asks: "Is it what we are playing?"

"It" says: "No, it is not a game."

Eventually, someone guesses: "Is it something some animals are?"

"It" replies: "Yes, it is tame."

When a player guesses the original word or when he asks a question that "It" cannot answer with a rhyme, he becomes "It" and selects the next word.

GHOST

Ghost is an old and tried spelling game, still one of the best for any age group that can spell. Any number can play and space is no problem. It makes a fine car or bus game.

The players take turns calling out letters to build a word but each player tries to avoid *completing* a word of more than two letters. When a word ends on a player, he becomes first a G-of-a-Ghost, then an H-of-a-Ghost the next time he ends a word, an O-of-a-Ghost, and so forth, until he becomes a whole Ghost and is out of the game.

Suppose the first player calls "C," and the second "A." The third will earn a G-of-a-Ghost if he adds "P" and finishes "cap." He can avoid the penalty by adding "M," for instance (with "came" or "camp" in mind). If a player adds a letter that doesn't seem to belong, the next player can challenge him. If the first player can name a word, the challenger becomes a "G-" (or an "H-" etc. of-a-Ghost). If there is no word or it is being misspelled, the player challenged is penalized, and the challenger starts a new word.

In a large group, it may speed up the game to eliminate a player after two errors, the first branding him half-Ghost and the second a full Ghost.

The last player left wins.

Team Ghost

Divide a very large group of 10-year-olds into two teams. Line them up opposite one another or sit them in semicircles. Teams alternate calling out letters, so that a player from Team A says, "C," Team B says "R," Team A says "O," etc. A player earns a half-Ghost each time he completes a word.

The winning team is the one with the most "live" players left when time is called.

TEAKETTLE

Teakettle is a play-way of dealing with homonyms and homographs, words that sound the same, but differ from one another in origin, meaning and often spelling. Such combinations may be bear and bare, blue and blew, or trip (meaning to fall) and trip (meaning a short journey). Any number from 2 to 50 can play.

While one player ("It") is out of the room, the group decides on a word or set of words with multiple meanings. The player returns and tries to discover the words. The others make conversation, substituting "teakettle" wherever they would normally use one of the words decided upon. Suppose the set of words selected are "to, two and too." One player may say, "I put teakettle books on the table teakettle." Another adds, "Teakettle dogs went teakettle the house immediately." The third says, "The teakettle of them ran teakettle the house teakettle."

"It" may join in the conversation and try to lead the group toward a topic he considers helpful. Each of the players contributes one sentence until "It" guesses the words. The player who leads to the solution becomes "It."

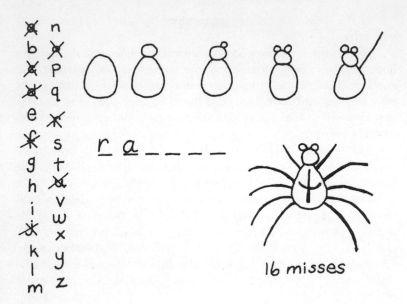

r a _ _ _ _

16 misses

SPIDER WEB

When you and I were young, we played a word game known as Hangman. For today's younger element, here is Spider Web, a less gruesome version that doesn't involve explanations about the role of hangmen.

It's a good paper and pencil game for two players, but converts easily to blackboard, wall or sidewalk play for many.

One player starts the game by choosing a word. He sets down one dash for each letter of the word. Off to the side, he writes down all 26 letters of the alphabet.

To make the game a little easier, he may supply classification (animal, plant, building, etc.) and possibly the first letter. For the 10-year-old, he may eliminate the first letter but indicate whether the word is a name, action or description (that is, noun, verb, adjective or adverb, etc.) .

If the word is "rabbit," for instance, he will hint it is animal and write: R - - - - -.

Each of the other players takes turns guessing the letters. Right guesses are written in on the proper dashes. Each wrong guess just crosses off a letter from the alphabet. For every such mistake, a part of the bug is drawn in — the head-thorax, the abdomen, four pair of legs, two pair of spinnerets, and perhaps two eyes. This gives the player 14 (or 16) misses before the Spider starts to spin his web.

The player who announces the correct word and fills in the last letter (or letters) chooses the next word.

CROSSWORD PUZZLES

Children's magazines and newspapers sometimes contain simple crossword puzzles that the young reader will enjoy solving. The homemade variety of crossword puzzle, however, has advantages. The puzzles can be geared to the particular reading and spelling level and to the special interests of the individual child or group.

Even the beginning reader will profit from puzzle-solving if you substitute pictures for verbal definitions, as in Diagram A. You will be amazed at the ingenuity of the neophyte in tracking down the spelling of a word. Picture dictionaries, reader vocabulary lists, and mother and father are among the usual sources, but one 6-year-old puzzle fan dug into the toy box for a long discarded game which he remembered had the word "elephant" written on it!

For the 9- and 10-year-old, the puzzle can be interrelated with literature, grammar, social studies, science, music and even mathematics.

Keep the puzzles short and don't worry about making them symmetrical. Rule off boxes (8 x 8 will do) and start in the upper left-hand corner. Fill in a word or two across and then work vertically as far down as the words go conveniently. Then draw a heavy line around the closest rectangle. Fill in black squares in the blanks and number the boxes. Then compose simple definitions for each of the words. Make copies for the children, with blank squares, of course, as in Diagram C.

Teach the 8-, 9-, or 10-year-old puzzle fan how to construct his own puzzles. It is as much fun to make the puzzles as it is to solve them and equally instructive.

For the first puzzles the children construct, it is better if they do not try to interlock words. Only when they are expert at this should they attempt the more complicated crossword puzzle shown in Diagram C. Initially, it will be sufficient challenge to try to find words and definitions to fit in one direction, as in Diagram B.

DIAGRAM -A-

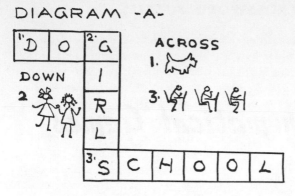

ACROSS
1. [dog image]
3. [children image]

DOWN
2. [girls image]

"D	O	²G
		I
		R
		L
³S	C	H	O	O	L

DIAGRAM -B-

¹M	Y
²M	A	N
³B	O	O	K
⁴H	A	P	P	Y
⁵M	O	T	H	E	R

Across
1. Belongs to me
2. Grown boy
3. Something to read
4. Glad
5. Parent

DIAGRAM -C-

¹B	²A	L	³L		⁴H
⁵O	N		⁶O	N	E
Y			O		N
		⁷S	K	Y

Across
1. A toy to bounce.
5. Put it -- the table.
6. 1 is spelled ---.
7. High in the ---.

Down
1. A brother
2. One
3. See
4. Mother of a chick

4. Mathematical Games

LEFT OR RIGHT

Left or Right is a game that helps to fix place and direction vocabulary, a necessary preliminary to mathematical learning. Any number can play.

The basic game is an old favorite, Hot or Cold. One child leaves the area or turns his back while the other players choose an object in the area for him to guess. Indoors, it could be a desk, a door, a book, a coat. Outdoors, it might a tree, a fence, a building, etc.

When the group recalls the player, he tries to guess the object. The others direct him toward the object with such words as: right, left, forward, back, over, under, near, far.

The 9- and 10-year-olds may limit directions to these: north, south, east, west, northwest, southwest, etc.

When the player locates the object, another member of the group takes a turn.

BEAN HUNT

Bean Hunt is a simple, active indoor game, combining the fun of a search with practical experience with quantities. It is particularly meaningful for the 6- and 7-year-olds. Provided you have the space, any number can play, but this is a successful diversion for a lone child, too.

While the children are away or have their backs turned, hide large beans throughout the room in as many different places as possible. Use dried lima or kidney beans, nuts (in their shells) or even small pebbles or paper clips. If necessary, make certain areas out-of-bounds for the hunters, but clear away anything that may suffer in the melee.

Then give the players an allotted time (5 minutes is usually ample) in which to find the beans.

When time is called, each player counts his find. The one with the most beans hides all the beans for the next hunt.

TOPSY TURVY

An understanding of size and shape is among the concerns of mathematics. Topsy Turvy is a new play-way of furthering those learnings. It can serve one or more.

Assemble a variety of empty cans, boxes, cartons and bottles, all with removable tops. Use baking powder, cereal and spice boxes; shoeshine and detergent cans, soda pop, syrup and medicine bottles; jelly, peanut butter and similar heavy jars. You should have a diversity of size and shape, with some varying only slightly in either size or shape.

Place your collection in an open shallow grocery carton or wooden box, with lids piled separately.

The task is to reunite box or bottle with its own top.

This can be a diversion for one, or you can set two or three to work in a race to see who does more within an allotted time. As each caps a bottle, he denotes ownership by placing his initials on it.

By Teams

If your group is large, provide a carton of bottles and lids for each team of 5 or 6. Seat each team in a circle about the carton. The leader hands a lid to the first player, who must locate the bottle, before picking up another lid which he hands to his right-hand neighbor. The second player on the team locates the bottle for his cover, picks up another lid and hands this to his right-hand neighbor, etc. The other team meanwhile is going through the same procedure with its bottles and lids. First team to finish scores a point.

If the contents of the cartons are not identical, teams exchange cartons before the next capping race.

First team to score 5 points wins.

Sets

If your child is into the New Math, you might use Topsy Turvy to demonstrate 1–1 correspondence between sets (a concept meaning a collection of related numbers, objects or ideas).

Assemble an assortment of boxes and jars and their lids. Eliminate one or two of either. Challenge the youngster to determine whether containers or lids are missing.

By merely counting each the child can determine which set is smaller, the set of containers or the set of lids. Once container and lid are matched, he can even indicate which elements are missing from the particular set.

NUMBERS

Usually played as an adult parlor game, Numbers can be just as much fun for the young ones, and good arithmetical exercise as well. It calls for a cleared room but any number from 10 to 40 can play.

Players count off to find the total number present. Then the leader calls: "Mix into twos." The group quickly separates into groups of twos. Anyone alone must drop out.

Then he calls: "Mix into threes," and the children scurry to form groups of threes. This time anyone who has not found two partners sits down. Next, perhaps, the call will be to: "Mix into fives."

The game continues for as long as the group is large enough for it to be fun.

A refinement for the 8-, 9- and 10-year-olds allows an isolated player to avoid dropping out by identifying himself, thus: "I am one-half of two" or "I am one-third of three." Two players can unite to announce: "We are one-half of four."

For the 10-year-olds, the leader may call: "Mix into groups of one-half of eight," and groups of fours form.

UP-TO-DATE

To familiarize youngsters with the calendar, introduce them to this new game. It is more fun as a relay but it converts to pencil and paper when necessary.

Divide the group into two or more teams of seven players. Label members of each team for one of the seven days of the week, and stand or seat players in order, with Sunday first.

Outline on a blackboard or a wall (hang up wrapping paper if you prefer) a chart composed of seven squares across and seven squares down. Across the top row fill in the current month and in the second series of horizontal boxes fill in the days of the week. Then with the help of the players, write the day's date in the proper box and circle it. You are ready to play.

The leader calls out a date. The players figure out on which day of the week it falls, and those labeled for that day race to write the date in the proper box. On our sample calendar, a call of "April 30th," for instance, would send players labeled "Thursday" scurrying to be first to write that date in the fifth box of the last horizontal row, as in the illustration.

As the calendar becomes more familiar, the leader might venture into last month and next month, and it is entirely fair to call: "Last day of the month," "Columbus Day," or "Day of the School Picnic."

Each time a date is filled in, credit one day of holiday to the team whose player first correctly fills in the date. First team to earn a two-week vacation wins.

PENCIL CALENDAR

Set this up for 1 or 41.

Distribute mimeographed calendar outlines, or direct each child to make an outline by folding paper. (To simplify this, have the child divide his paper into eight columns horizontally and vertically. The extra columns can be decorated appropriately.)

ALPHAMATH

Alphamath adds the intrigue of encoding and decoding to mundane math.

Possibly the simplest code is the following:

A	B	C	D	E	F	G	H	I	J	K	L	M	N	O	P
1	2	3	4	5	6	7	8	9	10	11	12	13	14	15	16

Q	R	S	T	U	V	W	X	Y	Z
17	18	19	20	21	22	23	24	25	26

"I am thinking of a four-letter word whose sum is 18," challenges the leader. First player to come up with an answer (example: head—8+5+1+4) gets a point and submits the next coded word, perhaps a two-letter word whose product is 105.

It's wise to confine the game to addition for younger players and to divide a group of 8 or 9 year olds into teams.

TICK-TOCK

Here's a new clock game, with variations that will provide challenges for even the more sophisticated 10-year-old. Groups of 13, 26 or 39 can play.

Togged out with cardboard or pie plates, each with a number from 1 to 12, twelve children stand in a circle to form a clock. All face in the same direction. A thirteenth child, the cuckoo, goes to the center of the clock face holding two dangling strings, one black to represent the hour hand and one red for the minute hand.

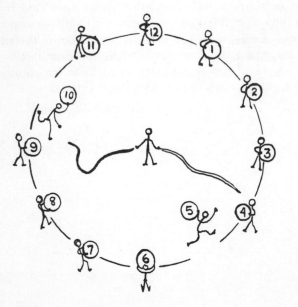

The leader calls "five o'clock." "5" dashes to the center to grab the black "hour hand" string, while "12" races for the red "minute hand" string. They run back with the strings to their positions in the circle. When the player in the center feels the strings are taut, he calls out: "Cuckoo!"

If the leader calls "ten after one," the players holding and "2" race for the strings. But if the leader calls "half six," one player, "6," would race for both strings. He would the "hour" string in the hand closer to the circle and "minute" string in the outside hand.

The game will get harder when the leader calls a nu that the children have to puzzle out, such as "five fifty-fi five to six." Then "6" and "11" must dash for the string

For the younger players, it is advisable to record, c back of the cardboard, the number of minutes after the their numbers represent. The child with "2" would ha minutes after" written on the back of the card; the chil "10" would have "50 minutes after or 10 minutes to" back of his card, etc.

If there are enough players to form two or more introduce the game to each clock before setting it in comp

Later

When the children really know how to tell time, yc try a few time problems, such as this one:

"It takes 20 minutes for Jane to get to school. S home at eight o'clock. What time does she get to sch

Before the game begins, each player fills in the name of the current month, the days of the week, and the day's date.

Then the leader asks a series of questions for which the calendar is needed to derive the answers. Here are some possible questions.

On what day of the week did the month start?

How many school days before our picnic on the 25th?

How many Sundays in this month?

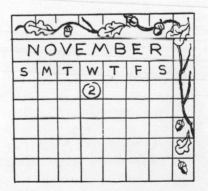

NUMBERS LINE UP

Once the rules of Numbers Line Up are learned, it can be a rough and tough romp in arithmetic. The children will be having too much fun to worry about "hating math."

Divide your group into equal teams of 4 to 10 players (it's better with 10) and designate a captain for each team. Each captain assigns to members of his team a number from 0 to 9. (If there are only 4 children on each team, he will assign numbers 0 to 3.) Then the captains hand out large pieces of oaktag or cardboard (paper will do but it often tears in the middle of the game). With one team using red crayons and the other using blue, each player writes his own number across the face of the cardboard.

The teams line up in numerical order at opposite ends of the room. The leader stations himself at a line drawn midway between the teams. Any children not playing serve as sorely needed referees and scorekeepers.

To warm up the game, the leader calls off a simple one- or two-digit number. He may call out: "Three." A player on each team holding "3" runs to the line and turns to face his team with his card in front of him. If the leader calls out: "Twenty," children with cards "2" and "0" run to the line and place themselves so that they read "20." First team to line up correctly scores a point.

Later when legs and minds are functioning, the leader may call out: "Four hundred ninety-two" or "Five hundred seven." When the game is really going, he may try a whopper like: "Eight million, six hundred twenty-four thousand, three hundred fifty-nine." Leader must remember not to call a double number like thirty-three because there is only one "3" to a team, and not to call high numbers if there are fewer than ten children to a team.

For the adept, he'll throw in a complication. "I'm adding these numbers: 2, 5, 9, 7, and I will subtract 3. Total?" First team to line up with the correct answer earns 2 points.

Classroom Numbers Line Up

Numbers Line Up has been played in an ordinary classroom, eliminating the running, and has proved *almost* as much fun. As many as 40 can play by dividing the group into four teams and stationing them in front, back and on the sides of the room.

Captains number members of their teams from 0 to 9 as above, and each player writes his number on a card or paper in the team color.

When a leader announces a number, players line up in order, and then either squat or sit. Supply chairs if you have the room — and the chairs.

Beginners' Line Up

Numbers Line Up is a much loved game among those 6- and 7-year-olds with whom we have played it. For most of this age group, it is better to restrict the numbers to three digits. Beyond the hundreds, most of them are lost.

After a while, try the adding problems, but combine only two numbers and keep the total below 10.

PLUS AND MINUS POTSY

Whether you set this one up as a sidewalk or floor game, or transfer it to a space-saving table, it provides painless experience with plus and minus symbols. It's also a good game to use to introduce signed numbers in algebra.

If it isn't convenient to chalk your floor or table, outline a diagram on wrapping paper or oilcloth with colorful crayon, paint or colored chalk. The simplest method is to draw a 2-foot square and mark it into nine 8-inch sections, three across and three down. Number the squares from 1 to 9 with large, bright figures. Tack or weight the diagram down flat.

For ground potsy, use two flat jar caps or two bean bags. Substitute a pair of Mason jar rings, washers, checkers, large plastic buttons or soda bottle tops for a table game. Chalk a plus sign (+) on one potsy and a minus sign (—) on the other.

Mark a starting line or toss mark about 3 feet from the diagram (less if it's table-bound).

Each player tosses the two potsies. He adds the score made by the plus potsy and subtracts that made by the minus potsy. A potsy landing on a division line does not score, and those which fall outside the square are minus 10. Winner is the player with the highest score after an agreed number of turns.

Teams' Plus and Minus Potsy

If there are four or more players, you can divide your group into teams. To handle more than 20 children, it is best to set up two diagrams and split the group into four teams.

Teams alternate tossing. Each player adds his score to his team total, checking his figures with an official scorekeeper from the opposing team.

Champion team is the one with the highest score after each player has had one turn.

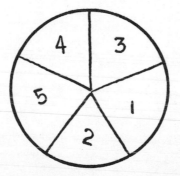

Beginners' Plus Potsy

The 6- and 7-year-old will enjoy playing a simplified form of arithmetic potsy. The diagram should contain only figures 1 through 5, and both potsies should be labeled with a + mark. Teams should be limited to two or three players.

One good diagram for this game is a circle with a diameter of about 2 feet. Divide it into five parts and number each section from 1 to 5. Place each child about 18 inches from the diagram. Each player tosses two potsies, one at a time, and adds the two numbers. He writes the total on a scorecard. (There is no rule against the group leaders supplying a little help with the scoring.)

Limit the number of turns to two for children playing as individuals, and to one for team members. After that, the computations get a little too involved for fun.

After the young ones work up some confidence, you can gradually increase the numbers on the diagram to 9. You will be surprised how easily these novices toss off the more difficult combinations, all in the interest of playing the game.

For the Whizzes

Substitute one potsy with a multiplication sign (✕) and one potsy that is blank. Sometimes players spend more time figuring than tossing, but none seem to mind.

BUZZ

Buzz is the perfect game for teaching and reviewing the multiplication tables. It needs no equipment and can be played anywhere. A whole classroom of 10-year-olds will find Buzz exciting, but for the 6- and 7-year-old, it is necessary to limit the group to three or four players. For this young age, it is most successful when played by an adult and one or two children.

Introduce Buzz by playing Buzz Five. The children take turns counting. The first player counts "one," the second "two," the third says "three," the next "four." Instead of "five," the next player substitutes "buzz." The counting continues with players saying "buzz" whenever there is a number containing the digit five, or a multiple of five. When players reach 50, they say: "buzz-buzz, buzz-one, buzz-two, buzz-three, buzz-four, buzz-buzz, buzz-six," etc.

When a player says the number instead of "buzz" or when he says "buzz" at the wrong time, he is out and the game goes on without him.

Go on from successful Buzz Five to Buzz Three, Buzz Four, and eventually even to Buzz Seven.

CIRCULAR SENSE

Rainy day fun at home or an excuse for more practice in class is provided by variations of Circular Sense.

Using the numbers given below, make each of the four rows of three numbers add up to 33 by writing one of the numbers in each circle: 5, 7, 9, 11, 13, 15, 17, 19

CLUE: Write the larger numbers on the outer circles.

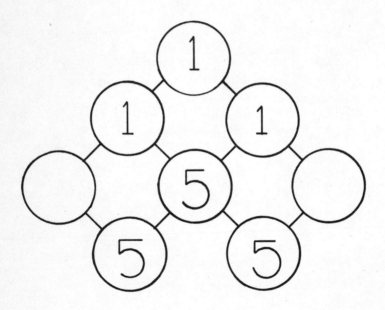

COIN CHECKERS

While two or four players are busy with checkers, make a Coin Checker board for the odd man out. Just outline eight circles in the order indicated in the diagram.

Place a small coin (or small white button) on each of the three circles marked 1. Place a larger coin (or black button) on each of the circles marked 5. The aim is to make the ones and fives change places before time runs out (three minutes or less).

Fives must *always* move upward and ones must *always* move downward.

If all three want to play Coin Checkers, just make three boards — and each plays on his own board. Winner then is the one who succeeds first.

GALLONS

Gallons is a variation of a favorite outdoor team relay involving carting water to and fro. With the use of standardized containers, the relay provides fun-filled experience with liquid measures. Provided you clear away *everything* that can be harmed by getting wet, Gallons might also be played in any room (even an ordinary classroom). From 8 to 16 can play on each team and you can have as many teams as you can provide room for.

In preparation, you will need to collect for each team the following: a one-gallon pail or empty paint can; four one-quart milk cartons (no bottles, please); and one half-pint container.

Set the empty quart cartons at one end of the room and the gallon pails full of water near the other end, as in the illustration. Each team lines up behind or at the side of one of the gallon pails.

The first player on each team is given a half-pint container. At the signal, he dips into the pail, fills the container and walks as fast as he can (without spilling the water) to his team's quart cartons. He empties his container and races back to hand it to the next player. It will take 16 such trips to empty the pail and fill the four quart cartons.

There is no reason why one player may not make more than one trip if there are not 16 players on each team.

To shorten the game (and give experience with pint measurement), you may substitute pint containers for the half-pint ones, thus requiring only eight trips to fill the cartons.

The first team to finish wins, but the quart cartons must be reasonably full. (The losing team mops up.)

If players are still raring to go, reverse the procedure. Supply any water missing from the quart cartons and set the players racing to empty the cartons (via the half-pint containers) and to fill the pail.

Quarts for Beginners

Simplify this relay for the 6- and 7-year-old by eliminating the gallon pail. Place empty quart cartons on one end of the room and full ones on the other. Supply each team with a cup or half-pint container. The task is to empty the full quart and fill the empty quart.

Try a wide-mouthed one-ounce bottle as dipper with which to fill a pint (or quart) carton.

GIANT STEP

Giant Step (also known as May I?) is a game that our parents and possibly our parents' parents played when they were children. With a little refurbishing, it serves well to teach children to judge distance, a skill so sadly lacking in many adults.

The game can be played outdoors or in a gym or room at least 50 feet long. From 6 to 25 players can play at any one time.

As originally played, a leader stood on the goal line facing the other players. The players lined up across the starting line, and each player in turn asked, "May I take some steps?" The leader then answered, "Yes, you may take 5 giant steps" or "Yes, you may take 3 baby steps," or "No, you may not."

Our newfangled leader has a helper with a yardstick. The leader says, "Yes, you may move ahead just 8 feet," or "Yes, you may take 6 inches," or "You may move 1 yard — back." The trick is for the walker to make an accurate move. If he does not approximate the instructions, he must go back to the starting line.

As in the original game, the other players may attempt to inch forward without being seen by the leader. If the leader catches anyone moving without permission, that player, too, must go back to the starting line.

The first player to reach the goal line becomes leader the next time the game is played. The player closest to the goal line becomes his assistant with the yardstick.

Practice Session

Children will soon learn the length of their pace by playing the game but if it seems necessary, or if the children want it after a bit of playing, you can give a small practice pacing lesson. Each child counts the number of steps it takes him to cover the playing area by walking from starting line to goal or from goal to starting line. By dividing the length of the playing area by the number of steps, he can determine how far he walks with each normal step.

AFRICAN THINKING GAME

An explorer goes to Africa to find his friend Diamala, but he doesn't know what tribe Diamala belongs to. There are three tribes in the area, the Elephant Tribe, the Leopard Tribe and the Crocodile Tribe.

A person belonging to the Elephant Tribe always tells the truth. A person belonging to the Leopard Tribe always lies, and a person belonging to the Crocodile Tribe sometimes tells the truth but sometimes lies.

In order to find his friend Diamala, the explorer must find out what tribe Diamala belongs to. He asks three Africans— Agassu, Bantu, and Coffi—two questions: "What tribe do you belong to? And what tribe does Diamala belong to?"

Agassu answers: "I am not an Elephant. Diamala is a Leopard."

Bantu says, "I am not a Leopard. Diamala is a Crocodile."

Coffi says, "I am not a Crocodile. Diamala is an Elephant."

What tribe does Agassu belong to? What tribe does Bantu belong to? What tribe does Coffi belong to? And finally what tribe does Diamala belong to?

(Solution on Page 119)

broadcast: 'The present temperature is 39° above zero, a rise of 5° since 8:00 A.M.' Was the 8:00 A.M. temperature 44°, 34° or 16°?''

TAKE YOUR PICK

Two children will find this fun. Eventually, one or both will be involved in figuring and the results will not be left to chance.

Mark out 16 lines on a slip of paper, as in the diagram. Players take alternate turns and each must cross out 1, 2 or 3 lines at each turn. The winner is the one who crosses out the last line.

/// /// /// /// ////

THE LAST STRAW

Here is another contest for two that can be played with straws, toothpicks or again with pencil lines.

Arrange 12 straws (or other items) in 3 rows, so that the top row has 5, the middle row has 4 and the bottom row has 3, as in the diagram.

Each player may take as many straws as he wants from any *one* row at a time. This time, the one left with the last straw is the *loser*.

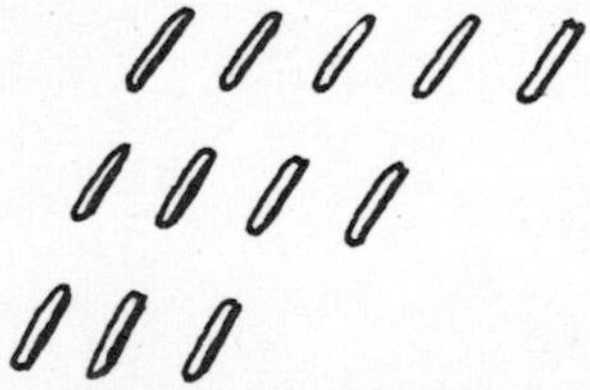

/ / / / /
/ / / /
/ / /

MATH MAGIC

With the allure of "magic," sums are reckoned with speed and accuracy. Teach this lightning calculation to the 7- to 10-year-old and see with what ease he plays it — with all who will.

Your young magician asks his audience to write down two rows of figures, each containing five digits, such as:

    1st: 3 4 6 5 8
    2nd: 4 6 8 2 9

The magician then puts down a third row of figures:

    3rd: 5 3 1 7 0

He asks the audience to put down a fourth:

    4th: 6 2 3 5 3

The magician writes a fifth row:

    5th: 9 7 6 4 6

Then the magician looks at the figures a moment and writes on a small piece of paper. He folds the paper and gives it to one of the audience to hold. He then asks the audience to add up the numbers and call out the total. When this is done, the young magician calls for his slip of paper and unfolds it. On it is written the correct total!

The wily magician had done his calculations while he was putting down his row of figures. When he wrote the third row, each number totaled 9 when added to the number *just above* it in the second row. (He ignored the top row.) In the fifth row, each number totaled 9 when added to the numbers in the fourth row.

The grand total could then be figured out very quickly from the *first* line — by subtracting 2 from the last number of the first line and placing 2 in front of the first number.

  Audience: 3 4 6 5 8
  Audience: 4 6 8 2 9
  Magician: 5 3 1 7 0
  Audience: 6 2 3 5 3
  Magician: 3 7 6 4 6
               ————————

GRAND TOTAL: 2 3 4 6 5 6

Exceptions

In the event that the audience writes a *first* number that ends in either 0 or 1, it will be necessary for the magician to mentally reverse the first and second row of figures. When he puts down the third row, he puts down numbers that total 9 when added to the numbers in the *first* row. He ignores the second row until the grand total. The procedure is the same as usual with the fourth and fifth rows. But the grand total is figured by using the *second* line — subtracting 2 from the last number and placing 2 in front of the first number.

Audience:	3	4	6	5	0
Audience:	4	6	9	2	9
Magician:	6	5	3	4	9
Audience:	6	2	3	5	3
Magician:	3	7	6	4	6

GRAND TOTAL: 2 4 6 9 2 7

5. Nature Study and Science Games

BIRD HUNT

To familiarize youngsters with the names of birds, organize a hunt. Any number from 5 to 40 can play.

Pin a picture of a bird and its name on each player's back. Try to include a variety of familiar and lesser-known birds — perhaps a gull, loon, grebe, heron, hawk, pheasant, finch, tanager, hummingbird, thrush.

Provide each player with a pencil and paper and send him to the hunt. The object is to find out the names of as many birds as possible, but each player tries to avoid having his own back seen while he tries to see the other names. No one may stand still with his back against any object.

When the birds are better known, cover the names of the birds and let the hunters identify them by their pictures alone.

Winner is the hunter with the longest list.

You can substitute animals, fish or plants, for variety and added learning.

TREELESS TREE-TAG

Tree-tag is a simple variation of an ageless running game. As in plain tag, a player called "It" chases the others to try to tag someone, who in turn becomes "It." But in tree-tag, the runners can escape by first touching the kind of tree previously agreed upon. Of course, this involves being able to identify an oak or maple or pine.

To adapt tree-tag for a treeless yard or gymnasium, plant pictures of trees at strategic spots, tacking or pasting them in place. For the game to be of any learning value, the illustrations must be accurate with characteristic bark, leaf, fruit, etc., clearly depicted. Several types of trees should be "planted" so that the children will actually have to look before touching. The variety of tree that is "safe" should be changed frequently, too. A runner cannot be tagged if he puts one foot on the proper tree on the floor or one palm on a tree against the wall.

Art Project

Children often enjoy preparing the trees for "planting." With the use of reference books, a committee of those interested can draw the required trees on 8 x 10 oaktag or cardboard. No titles should be allowed.

Variations

An illustration of a single leaf or other significant characteristic can be substituted for the whole tree, as an added challenge to the runners and to "It." Most of these can easily be chalked in on the ground or gym floor.

Immunity can also be granted by other plant life, or else particular rocks and minerals, and possibly even by sea shells.

SCAVENGER HUNT

An excellent outdoor nature study game, Scavenger Hunt can serve as a satisfying indoor pastime, too. Supplement your nature collection with a pile of nature magazines and reference books. "If you can't find the object itself, find a picture," is the direction to give to the players.

Prepare a list of things to be found — say a maple leaf, a piece of granite, a cocoon, a fly, a caterpillar, a bird's nest, an apple seed, a wildflower, a seashell, etc.

Just be sure that you have a specimen or a picture of each item. Write a separate slip for each item and place them in a bowl.

Let each player draw a slip and allow five minutes for the items to be found. If the specimen isn't portable, the player just indicates its location. If the object is in a magazine or book, he writes down the name and the page number on which the object can be found.

LITTLE ACORN

Little Acorn is a matching game based on a child's interest in the young of all species of animal and plant life. Use pictures or drawings, or specimens when available, of the mature animals or plants and their young (egg, larva, seed, flower, etc.). You may include the caterpillar and moth, tadpole and toad, acorn and oak, egg and bird, maggot and fly, calf and bull, etc.

Use separate cards for mounting each picture, or envelopes for inserting the specimens. At least for the first few games, label both pictures and specimens.

Divide the group into two teams — the "adults" and the "infants" — and hand out one card or envelope to each of the players. After a few minutes for inspection, the hunt is on. The object of the game is for players to pair off correctly according to species. If an "adult" locates an "infant" and says, "You're mine," the adult team scores a point. If an infant finds the adult first, he scores a point for his team. A player who matches incorrectly loses a point for his team.

When all the parents are matched with their children, the team with the most points wins.

BIRD, ANIMAL, FISH

Adapt this old favorite for any trio of categories. Any number from 6 to 40 can play, but a larger group makes for a better game.

Players form a circle. "It" walks around inside the circle and calls "Bird, beast or fish." Then, tossing a knotted handkerchief or paper-bag ball, "It" names one of the categories, such as "Bird!" The player tapped by the handkerchief must give the name of a bird before "It" can count to ten. If a bird is named, "It" must try again. When a player fails to answer in time, he becomes "It." Players may not repeat a name.

BLINDMAN'S BUTTON

Blindfold two players and then place each before a separate pile of buttons, screws, clips, beans and bobby pins. The first child to assort his pile correctly contends with the third child, and the winner of that match plays the next child, etc., round-robin fashion.

To secure his crown, the champion must correctly assort a button collection consisting of all the buttons from the two piles. He may select size or material as his classification.

MISMATCH

More observant than adults, children nevertheless don't always see the obvious. A group from 10 to 40 can have fun with Mismatch, testing both their ingenuity and their powers of observation.

Divide the group into teams and let the leaders choose for the first team to Mismatch. The losing team (the Observers) leaves the room. The Mismatchers get busy: they exchange socks, put ties on sleeves, bobbie pins on boys and boys' shoes on girls, bundle up in a raincoat, etc. If it is feasible, they can do a mismatching job on the room, too — a picture upside down, a chair on the desk, the clock reset. Time is called at the end of 5 or 10 minutes.

Then the Observers return. They spot as many of the Mismatches as they can within an allotted time (five minutes is usually ample).

If scoring is desired, a point is given for each correct observation. Mismatchers point out any oversights. A point is subtracted for each.

After a short period for righting the wrongs, the Mismatchers become the Observers and leave the room so that the other team can devise its own Mismatches.

Try older children on "Insect, Reptile, Mammal" or "Animal, Vegetable, Mineral."

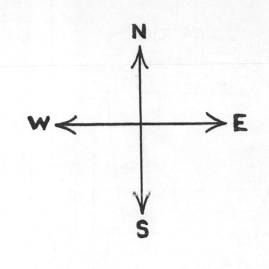

WEATHERVANE

To review the points of the compass, use this simple Weathervane.

The group stands in a body facing one player who serves as the Wind. The Wind indicates his pleasure by calling: "The wind blows . . . north." Quickly the players turn to the side or corner of the room that the direction indicated. If they are already facing north, anyone who changes position is out.

At first the Wind may help by turning with the group, but subsequently he may confuse the group by twirling and temporarily stopping in the wrong direction. Anyone misled is out.

After the game is thoroughly understood, halfway points such as northwest and southeast can be selected.

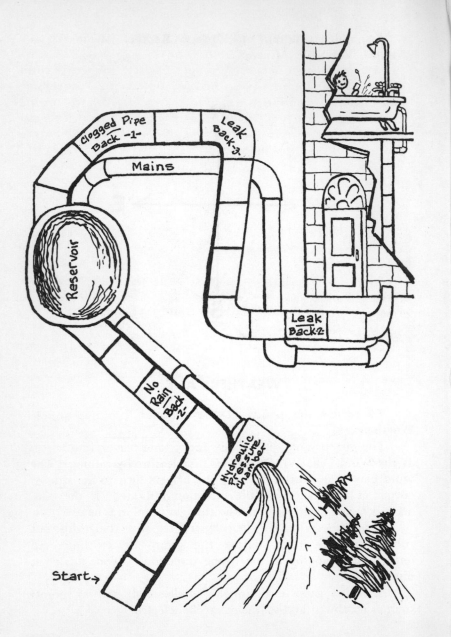

TONY TAKES A BATH

Parcheesi-type games can do much to make the young
understand the complexity of the operations behind the
fact that water runs from a faucet, that a switch turns
electric light, that a gas jet supplies fire for cooking. Y
make a game board for each of these stories and others.
four children can play on any one board at one time.

Outline the story on plain paper, cardboard, or, fo
durability, on wallboard or plywood. Go over the penc
with India ink or poster paint, and coat it with varnish or
if you wish.

If you tell the story of Tony Takes a Bath, for instan
the water from the mountains down a stream. Then t
through a hydraulic pressure chamber, through a pipe
reservoir, and from there through main pipes to a bra
Tony's house and up to his second floor bathtub.
obstacles in the form of dearth of rain, clogged pipes
leaks, and advantages in the form of heavy rainfall.

With a goal of getting from mountain stream to tu
player in turn spins a dial to learn how far to procee
different colored buttons for each player.

UP IN THE AIR

All in the interest of seeing how air lifts weight, the young scientist, aged 8, 9 or 10, will enjoy playing this game.

Pit two players against one another, arming each with a paper bag and a supply of books. Each player lays the paper bag flat on a desk or table and covers it with a book. The object is to blow up the bag, thus lifting up the book. Then a second book is added and the bag is blown some more. The winner of the contest is the player who can lift the most books with air.

WHEELS

A wheel reduces the friction caused by dragging an object across the room, and friction, as you know, affects the efficiency of moving bodies by causing heat.

This simple game demonstrates the difference between the work involved in dragging and rolling. It can lead readily to a discussion of wheels, friction, ball bearings, and so forth. Since the same game can be played again and again, there are infinite opportunities for review and further exploration of the same and related subjects.

You will need two cans — medium sized (#5) cans or larger are good for table or desk. Oil drums or small barrels are better if you have a large room or gym.

Divide the group into two equal teams, and station them at one end of the room or table. The entire length of the table or floor can be used.

The first players of each team start the race. With their cans or barrels in an upright position, they must push them to the goal line. They push the upright can with one finger if it is a table game. Then they turn the can on its side and roll it, again with one finger for the table game, to the starting line.

The second players follow the same procedure, pushing one way and rolling the other, and then the third players take over, until each member of each team has had a chance. Winner of the game is the team that finishes first.

In the meantime, each child has had an opportunity both to push and roll the same object.

WHEEL QUIZ

Here's a quiz game about wheels which makes a fine follow-up to the preceding game. Divide the group into two equal teams. In the manner of a spelling bee, members of opposite teams in turn name an application of the wheel, such as car, truck, skate. Anyone who can't think of an application that has not been named sits down. Winning team is the one with the most players standing when time is called.

At first it will be easy with such further examples as bicycle, wheelbarrow, dolly, tractor, motorcycle, grocery cart, but it will be the observant child who adds ferris wheel, merry-go-round, clothesline, water wheel, steering wheel, egg beater, phonograph, pencil sharpener, doorknob, wringer, clock gears, and so forth.

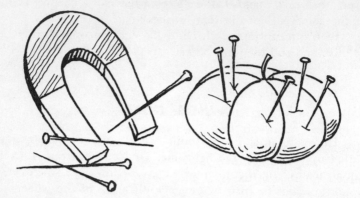

MAGNETISM

Anticipate a discussion of magnets and magnetism by putting a toy horseshoe to work. One or many participate in this useful game.

You will need a small horseshoe magnet, a supply of pins, and a pincushion or old sock for each child. Using a magnet, each player must pick up his pins and insert them, one by one, into the pincushion. When time is called, the player with the most pins in the cushion is the winner.

The game will lead easily to the work done by large magnets — lifting steel girders and beams — and to the linking of electricity and magnetism in the electromagnet to lift locomotives, automobiles, etc. From there on to the bell, the telegraph, and so forth.

STATIC ELECTRICITY

Before or after a discussion of static electricity, play the game of Static Electricity. Any number can participate in this fun-filled practical demonstration.

Divide the group into two teams. Station them near a wall on opposite sides of the room. Then hand to each player a balloon and string. Each is to blow up the balloon, secure it with string, and then rub it on a wool rug, cloth or woolen clothing to create enough static electricity to fix it to the wall. Time is called within 5 minutes. Winning team is the one with the largest number of balloons clinging to the wall.

SOUND THROUGH SOLIDS

To demonstrate how sound travels through solids, teach the children how to construct and operate a string telephone. Punch a hole through the center of the bottom of two open tin cans. Put cord through the holes and tie a knot at each end. You can wax the string to make it more rigid. With the string stretched taut, two children can talk to one another across the length of the room or through a closed door. The taut string carries the vibrations of the can to the ear.

Telephone Number

Once the telephones are made, use them to play Telephone Number, a game calculated to give practice in number recall. Divide the group into twosomes to man the telephones. Prepare several written lists of telephone numbers — 10-year-olds can make their own lists from a telephone directory.

Each child takes a turn at the transmitter reading off the telephone numbers. After each number, the other player, at the receiver, tries to repeat it accurately. After three mistakes, the players trade positions.

PHENOMENA

Phenomena masquerades as a guessing game but it is a stimulating new science game which encourages the players to recall what they have learned and find new applications. It requires a large group of 9- or 10-year-olds.

The group is divided into teams. One team leaves the room while the other selects and discusses a natural phenomenon, such as air, water, sound, light, heat, electricity, magnetism, the atom, rain, snow.

When the guessing team returns, each member is entitled to ask of any one member of the other team, "What do you do?" An appropriate, different answer must be given each time the question is asked. If air was selected, for instance, answers might include: "I lift airplanes," "I run factories," "I carry sound," "I keep a fire burning," "I help you to live."

If any member of the challenging team cannot answer the question, he must disclose the phenomenon. In that case, or if the guessing team figures it out by the time all members have answered the question, the guessers select the next phenomenon.

SOLAR SYSTEM

Your space-minded children will take readily to the Solar System Game. You will need at least 10 to play.

Label pie plates with the names of the sun and nine planets. As a reminder (or for the uninformed), place information about the particular planet on the back of the pie plate. The data might include distance from the sun, size, temperature, gases, etc. It would be wise for the leader to have a master copy of the information.

Give out the pie plates to the members of the group. Give each player a chance to discuss the information on his plate. After all have told what they know of their planet, the leader calls, "Line up by distance from the sun." The children must then arrange themselves according to their distances from the sun: Mercury nearest, then Venus, Earth, Mars, etc. The leader might follow with, "Too cold to harbor life." The planets that are too cold would step forward.

The leader might then ask "Line up by size."

For this game you might award a star for each correct response.

6. Social Science Games

THIS IS WHAT MY DADDY DOES

To children just beginning to be aware of the world of work outside their home, daddy's business or job is a source of curiosity. This game gives an opportunity for each child to share the information he has acquired about his own parent's work — or to acquire that information if he has not already done so.

The leader or a volunteer starts this way:

"This is what my father (or mother or uncle) does! Name it if you can."

The leader then acts out an occupation. For example: he turns to ask a question, pushes down a meter flag, drives a car, helps a passenger out, accepts money, gives change.

The others guess and the one who comes up first with "taxicab driver" acts out the next job.

Often, this game serves as a stimulus to learn more about what's involved in a particular trade or profession. Even the child who knows his parent is a salesman or a lawyer or an engineer may not know what he *does*.

AMBITIONS

When it is advisable to involve the children in physical activity, divide the group into teams and play Ambitions.

One group withdraws and decides on a future trade or occupation and returns to chant:

"Watch us now if you'd be shown,
What we shall be when we are grown!"

The other group responds:

"What'll you do? What will you be?
Show us now so we can see!"

Then the first group acts out their occupation: players slide down a pole, throw on raincoats and helmets, jump onto a fire engine, hang on through traffic, start unloading hoses, etc. They want to be firemen.

If the other team guesses, they retire to decide on their own future. If they fail to guess, the same team has another opportunity.

In a gym, the guessing can be followed by a chase of the ambitious ones by those guessing. Anyone caught joins the rival team.

THE FARMER GROWS THE WHEAT

To the tune of "The Farmer in the Dell," this singing and pantomime game helps youngsters aged 6, 7 and 8 to learn the story behind the slice of bread they eat. The larger the group the better.

It is wise to explain to the players not only the motions that accompany the words but the reason why the farmer digs or the miller grinds. You can introduce the technical vocabulary — plowing, harrowing, harvesting, threshing, etc.

The entire group forms a circle, but the 6- and 7-year-olds, and most 8-year-olds, enjoy having an individual child singled out to act as farmer, miller, baker, grocer and child, and to lead the group in the pantomime.

WORDS	PANTOMIME
1 The farmer grows the wheat	Digging, planting, cutting, threshing (flailing)
2 The millers grind it to flour	Windmill turning, grinding, sifting, filling flour bags
3 The baker makes the dough	Mixing, kneading, dough rising (follow with hands), and putting in oven
4 The grocer sells the bread	Taking off shelf, packing, taking money, saying thank you
5 The child eats the slice	Just eating — or asking mother, making sandwich, then eating

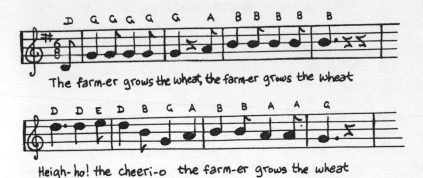

The farm-er grows the wheat, the farm-er grows the wheat

Heigh-ho! the cheeri-o the farm-er grows the wheat

LAND, SEA, AIR

Land, Sea or Air is designed to help the 6-, 7- and 8-year-olds increase their knowledge of the many transportation vehicles.

The leader stands in front of the group and chants: Land, Sea, Air . . . Land, Sea, Air . . . . He matches the words with movements of the hand: rolling, rowing, flying.

After several such chants, he calls out the name of a vehicle of transportation. He might, for instance, call, "Taxicab." The group must immediately roll hands to indicate it travels on land. Anyone who rows or flies is out.

Next the leader might call "Jet." All must fly. Anyone who rolls or rows is out.

At first, the leader will indicate the required movement but later he may keep his hands motionless or even make a confusing movment — that is, fly when he should be rowing, etc. However, whenever he introduces an unfamiliar vehicle, the leader makes sure to pantomime correctly.

DATE RATE

Because the months of the year are of peculiar fascination but often cause amusing confusion, especially for the 6- to 8-year-old, Date Rate will prove a most popular pastime. Any number can play.

The players can form a circle or just sit down at random. In a classroom, it is satisfactory for the children to remain in their seats.

As the leader or a volunteer moves in and out among the players, he chants, slowly or quickly as he prefers, the following:
"Don't be late,

A fact to state

About a date

In the month of ----."

At that point, the leader taps a player, shouts "September" or some other month, and then begins to count. Before he reaches 20 (10 for the 10-year-olds), the player selected must give a fact about the month named. He may state, "September has thirty days," "September is the first month of school," or "September is the ninth month of the year" or anything that is correct. If a player states a fact in time, he takes the leader's place. There is no rule against repeating the same month more than once but the same fact about the month may not be used again.

Date Rate for Two

By eliminating the perambulating "It," you can play Date Rate as a car game for parent and child. Allow birthdays and other personal anniversaries. After a bit, you have to be ingenious to think of another fact about the same old month. Ten-year-olds will enjoy a challenge to give as many facts as possible by the count of 20.

TELEPHONE CONVERSATION

In a few years, our youngsters will be teenagers and it will be difficult to get them *off* the telephone. As yet, however, the telephone is still a relative novelty for most. While they are still in this uninitiated stage, Telephone Conversation is a good game with which to introduce the conventions of telephoning, encourage content and brevity, and provide opportunities to dramatize familiar community facilities.

Two players are selected to carry on a telephone conversation, and are given a few minutes for planning. The conversation can be between storekeeper and customer, parent and teacher, housewife and plumber or electrician, or it can represent a call to the local fire department, police station, hospital or railroad station. The call, however, must have a purpose other than socializing.

Once the planning is completed, the conversationalists go to the telephone. Use imaginary, toy or homemade telephones. For an allotted time (3 to 5 minutes is usually ample), the children conduct the business at hand. In each case, they should follow telephone etiquette and cover the "who, why, where, when and how" of the situation.

Members of the group interpret the telephone situation and discuss possible short cuts and improvements.

Then the next two players plan a conversation.

WHO AM I?

This version of a popular game is calculated to encourage children to keep up with the news. Even the younger children listen to radio and television news before they are ready for newspaper reading! Any number can play.

Onto the back of each player, pin a card with a name in the week's news. Each player must learn who he is by asking questions that can be answered by "yes" or "no." If time is no problem, it is more fun to have the children take turns asking questions so that the group can listen in.

At first, it will be wise to restrict your guest list to front-page and possibly sports-page celebrities. Gradually, however, players learn to distinguish national, state and local figures, and foreign and domestic notables.

NECESSITIES

Children of 8, 9 and 10 are just beginning to learn that people everywhere have the same basic needs — food, clothing, shelter. To reinforce this learning, play Necessities. A larger group makes for a better game.

The players form a circle and one player sits in the center chanting: "Food, clothing, shelter." He spins a bottle on its side and calls, for instance: shelter. When the bottle stops, the player it points to must respond with an example, such as igloo, hut, log cabin, teepee, apartment house, and so on. He then goes to the center of the circle and selects the next category. If a player fails to answer, the same player continues as "It."

If clothing is called, the answer should indicate the material of which it is made, fur or fur coat (not merely coat), for instance. Similarly an example of food should indicate source — chicken egg, cow's milk, lamb chop, whole wheat bread.

SALE TALE

Apart from the things that a child buys for himself or buys on errands for his parents, most youngsters have confused and hazy ideas about the cost of living. Sale Tale should correct some misconceptions, and perhaps even curb a few "buy me" spells.

Prepare for the game by cutting out illustrated advertisements from newspapers and magazines, and possibly from mail order catalogues. These can be items of clothing, toys, groceries, tools, books, kitchen equipment, furniture, musical instruments, cars, boats, houses, and such services as transportation, entertainment, telephone, electric and gas, laundry, shoe repair, haircutting, etc. Don't choose misleading ads or special "bargains." The goal is not for the child to learn the difference between a $1600 car and a $2000 car, but, for instance, to discover that a car costs much more than a refrigerator, that air travel is more expensive than bus fare, that a particular toy costs as much as a pair of shoes.

Mask the price in each ad but be sure you will be able to remove the mask without tearing the paper. (Paste or tape down only the ends of the covering strips.)

If the group is large, you can divide it into "families" of 5 or 6, or "companies" of 10 or more.

The leader or "salesman" holds up an item and calls for estimates. Each family, company or individual is allowed one guess of the cost of the item. The cost is then unmasked and the individual or group who came closest to the real price is awarded the merchandise — the illustrated ad.

A "Competent Consumer" badge is awarded to the family, company or individual with the most illustrations at the end of the sale.

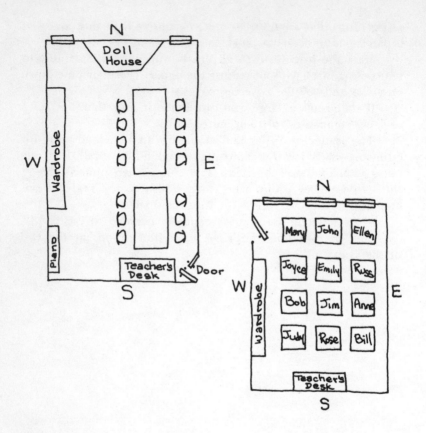

MAP GAME

A map is an unreal thing to a youngster. The best way to help him understand that a map *represents* a larger area is to set him to make a map of an area within his ken, an area he can envisage. The map of a room — a room plan — serves that purpose. Once it is made, it can be used for a map-reading game.

The 10-year-old can be expected to draw the map to size, with help if necessary. Measure or pace off the room. If it is

12 feet by 18 feet, for instance, show him how to scale it down to 6 inches by 9 inches. Then let him draw in the outlines of the room on a large sheet of oaktag, cardboard or wrapping paper. Help him to locate north so that he can make that side of the map the top, and then label south at the bottom, east on the right, and west on the left.

After this, fit in the doorways, windows and the large pieces of furniture. If it is a plan of a schoolroom, fill in the desks (and possibly indicate the names of the children who sit there).

When the map is finished, it may be mounted on cardboard and shellacked or varnished. It then serves as the board for the Map Game.

One player starts by directing others to name the article of furniture, for example, northeast of the window, or 3 feet from the door, or south of Mary. The first child to find and name it scores a point, and selects the next object or person to be located. Whoever first scores 3 points is the winner.

ROAD MAP

This game gives experience in the first type of map likely to be of practical use — the road map. Two or many can play.

Divide a large group into teams and give each small group a road map. Assign each a trip to take. They are to figure out the shortest way to get to their destination, outline the route in red, and give the number of miles.

You can score this by awarding a point to the team that completes the task first. Usually, however, this isn't necessary. The children become too engrossed in the map to care!

MASTER OF THE MAP

The 9- and 10-year-old will learn much and enjoy the process with this map-reading game. Two or more can play.

One player picks a place on the map, then names it for the others, and challenges them to find it within an allotted time. The one who locates the place selects the next, or if it is not found, the same player shows its location and gets another turn.

If the group is large, divide it into two teams. Teams alternate challenging the other to locate the town, city, state. Score a point for each place found. If necessary, the child who chose the place can help the guessers by telling them whether they're "hot" or "cold."

GEOGRAPHY

Introduce this old favorite to the 9- and 10-year-old. They'll enjoy the game but don't expect them to be whizzes at this age. Allow plenty of time for thought. From 4 to 40 can play.

One player starts the game by giving the name of a city. The next player must then give the name of any city, state or country beginning with the last letter of the city named.

If the first player names Boston, for instance, then the next might say New York. The third might come up with Kentucky, the fourth with Youngstown, and the fifth with North Dakota, and so on. No name may be repeated.

When a player can't think of a name beginning with the last letter of the one just given, he drops out of the game. The last one left is the winner.

EXPLORATION

This seemingly simple game captures the imagination of the 9- and 10-year-old and can stimulate independent research in a variety of fields.

Just divide the group into small teams and send each to an encyclopedia, history, geography, dictionary or atlas — to come up with an interesting discovery.

TELEPHONE TIME

Telephone Time is a fun-packed history game for the 9- and 10-year-old. Any number from 4 to 40 can play.

The group is divided into twosomes. Each pair quietly chooses any two historical characters or prominent living persons and prepares a conversation. The only rule is that the two be contemporaries.

They can be Columbus and Queen Isabella, George Washington and Benjamin Franklin, the President of the United States and Prime Minister of England, the Mayor and the Police Commissioner, a ballplayer and his new manager.

Before they start, the conversationalists indicate whether the telephone could have been used by their characters, or whether some other method of communication would have been necessary. They say, "We really sent our messages by . . ." and indicate courier, pony express, telegraph, etc. (They can consult the leader for this information if necessary.)

The conversation itself should not run more than a minute or two. During this time the two never mention each other's assumed names.

When time is called, the others guess the identity and situation. The player who guesses correctly goes up with his partner for the next conversation.

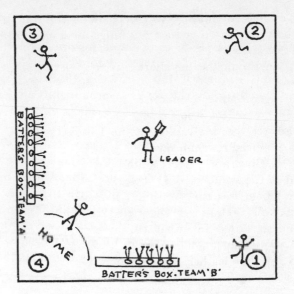

SOCIAL STUDIES BASEBALL

Social Studies Baseball actually adds a little physical activity to the who, where, what and when of geography, history and current events.

Divide the group into two equal teams. You need not worry about having exactly 9 players on each; the game plays as effectively with teams of 5 or 19. Team captains choose for first chance at bat, and assign a batting order.

The four corners of the room serve as the three bases and home plate. The team at bat sits or stands lined up near the batter's box. The other team sits on the other side of the room.

The first child in the batting order stands at home plate and is fired a question by the leader. If he answers the question correctly, he goes on to first base. No stealing is permitted. When three of his teammates have made hits by answering questions, the first player comes in to score. Any player who fails to answer correctly is out. After three outs the team retires for the inning, and the other team takes its place at the plate.

The number of innings will depend on the time allotted, but it is best to plan on at least 3 innings for a team of 9, and 6 innings for a team of 18.

Question should be the short-answer variety, such as these examples:

Who invented the telephone?
Where do we get wool?
Where was the first capital of the United States?
Who is Vice-President now?
Who is Governor of this state?
What is the name of our Mayor?
After whom was this continent named?
What holiday falls on October 12th?
Columbus sailed for what country?
What is cotton?
Who supplies leather for our shoes?

HEADLINE

Headline makes a copy editor of your 9- or 10-year-old to make sure that he really understands a news story. The game can be played by one or many.

Clip suitable stories from daily newspapers, weekly news magazines, and from special children's bulletins. Mask the headlines with removable tape, or snip them off and store them separately.

A story is passed to each of the players to read or, if the group is large, it is read aloud by the leader. Then each player composes a head or short title that he considers suitable for the story. These are read aloud, after which the actual headline is consulted.

WHERE AM I?

A deceptively simple game, Where Am I? is a challenging geography lesson for the 10-year-old.

One player imagines he is in a specific place. The others try to discover where by asking only questions which can be answered by "yes" or "no." With a little guidance the players learn to go from the general question to the more specific.

Are you in the Northern Hemisphere?

Are you on the North American continent?

Are you in the United States?

Are you on the Eastern seaboard?

Are you in one of the Mid-Atlantic states?

Are you in New York State?

Are you in a city?

Are you in the capital?

The player who guesses chooses the next place.

To make the game easier for the younger player, a hint is given such as: "I'm in the eastern part of the United States."

PERSON, PLACE OR THING

Person, Place or Thing is Guggenheim adapted for the 10-year-old. It's a provoking paper and pencil game for one or many.

Make a chart of a short word going down the left and three categories across the top, as in the diagram. You may substitute another word for *Life* but it should be equally brief. The players must fill in each category with a name beginning with each letter of the word. You can keep the Person, Place or Thing categories general, or specific as in the example.

Since this is a learning as well as a fun game, by all means give access to an atlas, dictionary, encyclopedia, history text, and any other reference material you have about. Chances are they'll be well used.

	PERSON *Americans*	PLACE *Countries*	THING *Foods*
L	Abe Lincoln	Luxemburg	lamb chop
I	Washington Irving	India	ice cream
F	Benjamin Franklin	France	frankfurter
E	Thomas Alva Edison	England	egg

PREDICAMENTS

Predicaments requires all the players to solve problems that arise in their child's world. A group from 4 to 40 can play.

One player leaves the room while the others decide on a predicament. The leader should help select the first one or two so that the children understand they are not to choose far-fetched situations. Here are some samples of the kind of predicament: discovering in a pocket a letter given to you to mail two days ago; getting on a wrong bus; being locked out of the house; being confronted by a strange, angry dog; fire breaks out in your house, and so forth.

"It" comes back into the room and asks each player in turn, "What would you do?" Each must give an *appropriate* answer, in effect a solution to the problem, while "It" tries to guess the predicament.

Thus while "It" is guessing the problem, the others are actually holding a discussion about a situation each may face.

The one who gives away the predicament is the next "It."

AFRICAN THINKING GAME SOLUTION

Since the person belonging to the Leopard Tribe always lies, Bantu must be a Leopard (because he says he isn't). And Diamala cannot be a Crocodile.

Since every member of the Elephant Tribe always tells the truth, Agassu (who says he is not an Elephant) cannot be an Elephant. He must therefore be either a Leopard or a Crocodile.

Since Bantu is a Leopard, Agassu is not a Leopard, but a Crocodile.

Coffi, therefore, must be a member of the Elephant Tribe— and Diamala must be an Elephant, too, because truthful Coffi says so.

INDEX